RAILROAD ENGINES
FROM AROUND THE WORLD
Coloring Book

BRUCE LaFONTAINE

DOVER PUBLICATIONS, INC.
MINEOLA, NEW YORK

About the Author

BRUCE LaFONTAINE is the writer and illustrator of thirty-five nonfiction books for both children (ages 8–12) and adults. He specializes in books about history, science, transportation, and architecture. His published works include *Modern Experimental Aircraft*, *Famous Buildings of Frank Lloyd Wright*, *Great Inventors and Inventions*, and others. His *Exploring the Solar System* (1999) was selected by *Astronomy* magazine as one of the twenty-one best astronomy books for children. *Astronomy* also selected his *Moon Exploration Fact and Fantasy*, published in 2001, as one of that year's ten best astronomy titles for the holidays. He is included in *Something About the Author* and the *International Biographical Centre Who's Who of Authors*. He has worked in the Rochester, New York area for twenty-five years.

Bibliographical Note

Railroad Engines from Around the World Coloring Book is a new work, first published by Dover Publications, Inc. in 2003.

International Standard Book Number

ISBN-13: 978-0-486-42378-4
ISBN-10: 0-486-42378-6

Manufactured in the United States by RR Donnelley
42378607   2015
www.doverpublications.com

INTRODUCTION

Railroad engines provide powerful, colorful, and enduring images of different cultural periods through the history of the industrial world. During their infancy in the early 1800s, these engines, or locomotives, were the largest and most powerful machines of their time (in this book the terms "railroad engine" and "locomotive" are used interchangeably). In Britain, where the steam locomotive originated, forward-thinking inventors continually improved on the first model and quickly popularized the idea of the railroad as a transporter of passengers as well as freight. The groundbreaking European concept made its way to the United States during the middle and later years of the century, with the "iron horse" soon becoming a symbol of westward expansion across the vast continent. The steam locomotive literally pulled the east and west coasts together: the ceremonial driving of a golden spike in the track at Promontory, Utah in 1869 marked the beginning of the transcontinental railroad system.

But the true golden age of railroad engines began around 1890 and lasted until the mid-1950s. During this period, there was no better symbol of technological progress and the rise of industrial might, especially in the United States. Driven by steam, electric, or diesel technology, fast, powerful streamlined railroad engines were the ideal image for the modern world and its bright future.

The physical principle underlying steam power has been understood for centuries. It is a property of water to expand to many times its original volume—1,700 times, to be exact—as it is heated and turned to steam. Controlling and applying the tremendous pressure created when steam is produced inside a closed chamber was the technological achievement of the late 1700s, when steam engines were developed into practical working machines. In these, the pressure of the expanding steam is exerted on a moveable piston inside a cylinder-shaped chamber, causing it to slide forward or back. A complex system of connecting rods, crankshafts, valves, and other mechanical gear transmits the power to the apparatus performing the function of the machine—in the case of a locomotive, the driving wheels resting on the track. In 1803, Richard Trevithick demonstrated his "steam engine on wheels" at the Penydarren mine in South Wales. His engine pulled wagons loaded with ten tons of coal over a metal track, or "railway," for a distance of nine miles. This was the beginning of the history of the railroad engine. Most of this book covers steam locomotives, since they comprise the most numerous type of engine in railroad history.

Steam locomotives of the early 1800s were relatively simple, small, and slow. Over the following 120 years, they evolved into sophisticated and powerful machines, some over 100 feet long, that were able to transport hundreds of tons of freight and passengers at great speeds.

The power of a railroad engine is measured in terms of "tractive effort," measured in pounds. This figure represents the machines' ability to pull a load with 85 percent of its steam pressure applied to the pistons. The lowest tractive effort described in this book is 450 lbs., that of the *Best Friend of Charleston*, built in 1830. The most powerful is that of the mammoth Union Pacific Big Boy, introduced in 1941. It produced a tremendous 137,500 lbs. of tractive effort.

During the golden age of railroads, some steam locomotives and the trains they pulled became famous with the general public. Long-distance express trains transported thousands of people daily and were given dramatic names like the *Broadway Limited, Hiawatha, Twentieth Century Limited,* and *Daylight*. But new technology was developing that would soon end the era of the steam locomotive. Around the turn of the twentieth century, electric locomotives began operation. They were run directly from overhead or underground power cables that fed electric traction motors used to drive the wheels. Beginning in the 1930s, diesel-electric locomotives were introduced. They used onboard diesel engines to run electric generators which fed power to electric traction motors at the wheels. Diesel-electric engines were powerful, fast, and reliable, and in a few short years their use was almost universal.

By the mid-1950s, the railroad industry in the United States was in a general decline that reflected the growing popularity of air travel and exploding automobile ownership and highway construction. Over the following twenty years, many of the nation's well-known railroads went out of business. In the 1970s, the U.S. Congress created two quasi-public corporations to maintain rail service: in 1971 it created Amtrak (National Railroad Passenger Corporation), which took over intercity passenger service, and in 1976 the freight carrier Conrail (Consolidated Rail Corporation), into which it merged most of the surviving roads. (Conrail was later sold into the private sector and is now owned jointly by CSX and

Norfolk Southern Corp.) In the late 1980s there was a resurgence of public interest in rail travel, due to rising airfares, traffic congestion at crowded airports, and, to some extent, nostalgia. The American passenger railroad system was, for a time, on the comeback trail, although its dependence on government funding has once again made its future somewhat uncertain; elsewhere in the world, of course, railroads have not been allowed to decline so greatly. Millions of travelers still depend on the far-flung Eurail system to visit more than twenty-five countries in Europe, using train types ranging from scenic to hotel-style. Many nations have developed sophisticated high-speed rail lines, with speeds in the 150–200 mph range, and Amtrak has recently put its new Acela trains into service on the heavily used Washington–New York–Boston route in the Northeast. Promising new technology for future high-speed rail travel is also being explored. Magnetic levitation *(maglev)* trains that could cruise at 250 mph or more, propelled and held above the track by powerful magnetic fields, have been under development since the 1970s. The world's first maglev railway line, using German-made equipment, is now being built in China.

Whatever happens, the exciting and colorful story of rail travel will continue, and its rich heritage of powerful technology and powerful images will continue to fascinate.

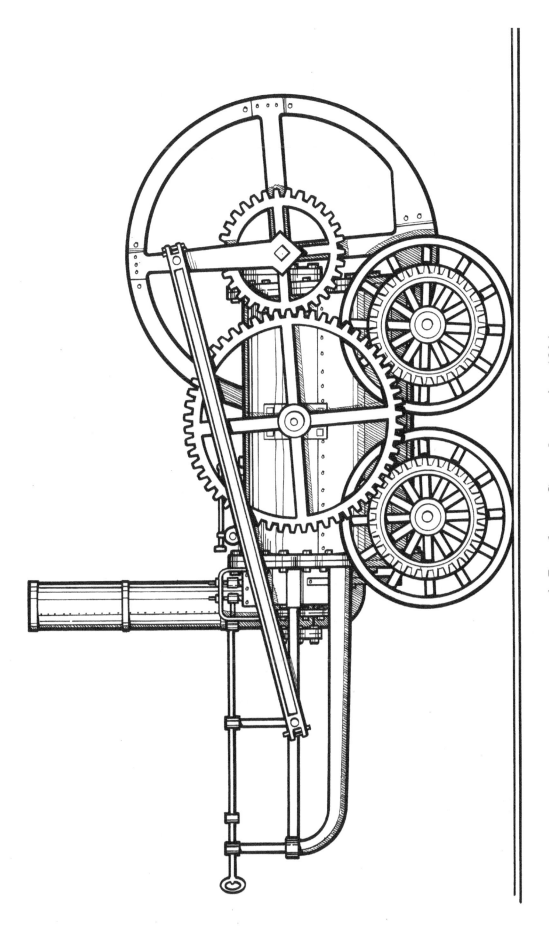

1. *Penydarren*. Steam locomotive, 1804

The first steam-powered locomotive to run on a metal track or "railway" was built in South Wales by the Cornish engineer Richard Trevithick, who had previously invented and built several steam-powered engines, including one on wheels that propelled itself along ordinary roads. In February 1804, he demonstrated the machine's ability to transport cargo by rail. The *Penydarren* hauled 10 tons of iron and seventy passengers in five cars from the Penydarren Ironworks near Merthyr Tydfil to the Merthyr–Cardiff Canal at Abercynon, a distance of nine miles. The *Penydarren* was never put into regular service—it made only three trips—but it successfully proved the potential of steam railroad engines to haul freight. In 1808, Trevithick built and operated on an enclosed circular track in London another locomotive which he named *Catch Me Who Can.* It was a minor sensation for a time, but at a shilling a ride, a little too expensive to achieve popularity with the general public.

Both *Penydarren* and *Catch Me Who Can* proved too heavy for the cast iron rails that were the strongest that could be made at that time, but these and other early steam engines inspired the inventors and engineers of the era to develop new and improved railroad technology.

2. *Puffing Billy.* Steam locomotive, 1813

The first locomotive to operate successfully on a commercial basis over metal railways was the *Puffing Billy.* This 7-ton engine had wheels without a metal flange, or lip, on the inside edge that prevented slipping off the track as did later locomotives; instead the track itself was flanged outward to hold the wheels in a stable position. *Puffing Billy* was built for the Wylam Colliery (coal mine) near Newcastle, England, and was used to haul coal from there to the River Tyne, a distance of 5 miles. It remained in operation until 1862.

Puffing Billy was built in 1813 by the engineer William Hedley. It was constructed of wood and iron with copper and brass fittings.

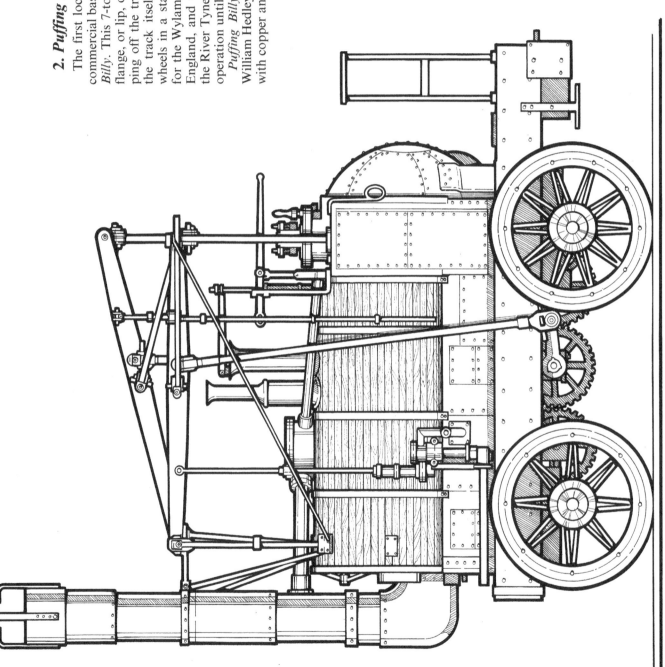

3. *Locomotion.* Steam locomotive, 1825

On September 27, 1825, a steam railroad engine aptly named *Locomotion* was inaugurated on the first public rail line, the Stockton & Darlington Railway, which served the coal mining district near Newcastle-on-Tyne in northern England. It was built by pioneering locomotive engineer George Stephenson. On its inaugural run it carried special passengers in a coach placed between two coal cars.

The Stockton & Darlington was a highly successful freight carrier, and at first, passenger traffic was carried only by private contractors using horse-drawn coaches on the railway line. In 1833, however, the company began its own passenger service, and the age of the passenger railway began. *Locomotion* was painted yellow and red and had fittings of iron, copper, and brass.

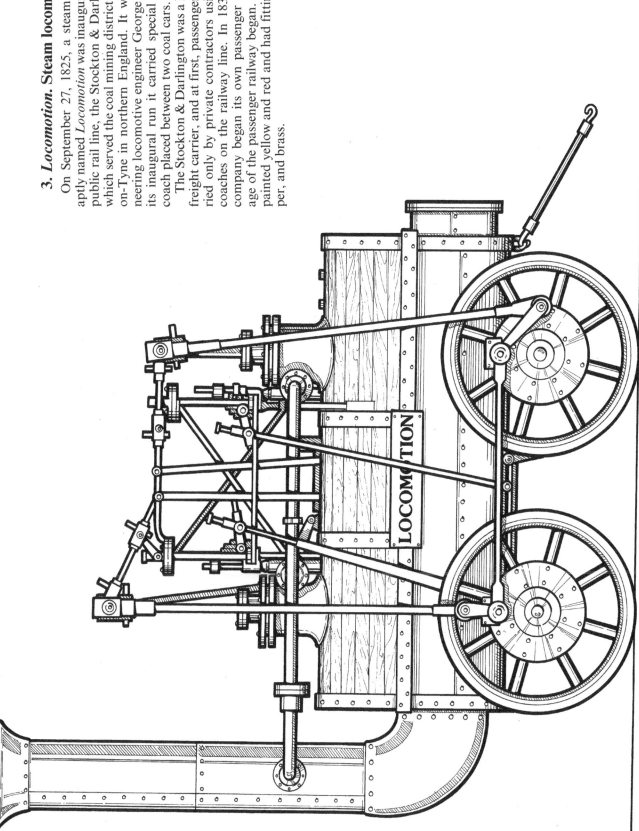

LOCOMOTION

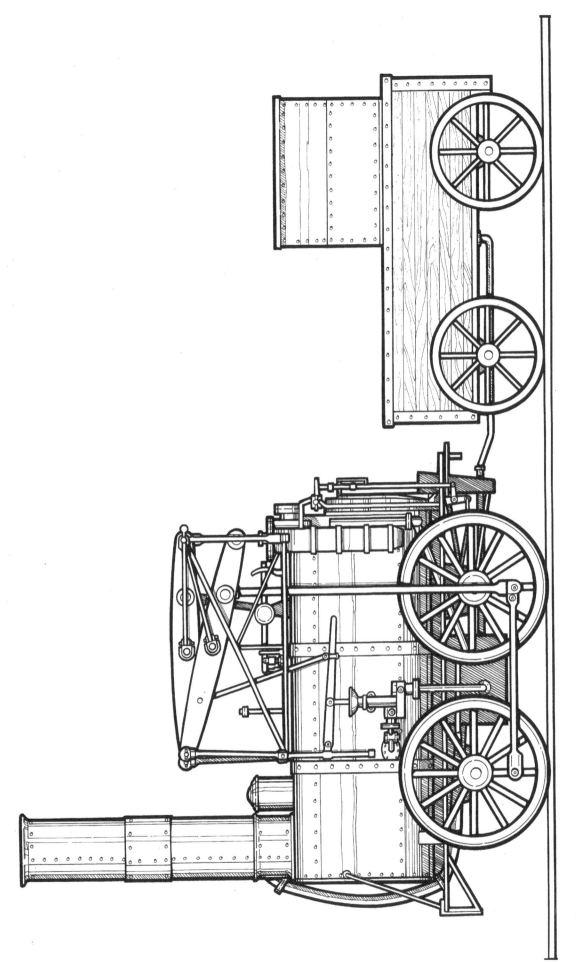

4. *Stourbridge Lion*. Steam locomotive, 1829

The first steam locomotive to operate in the United States was the British-built *Stourbridge Lion*. It was designed by the American engineer Horatio Allen to haul coal for the Delaware & Hudson Canal Company. It was built in 1829 by Foster, Rastrick & Company of Stourbridge, disassembled, and shipped to America with three other railroad engines. It was never put into regular service. The *Stourbridge Lion* was the only locomotive of the four actually delivered to the Delaware & Hudson. It was assembled at the West Point Foundry in Cold Spring, New York and tested successfully, at speeds up to 10 mph, on a 3-mile track that included a trestle bridge near Honesdale, Pennsylvania. It proved too heavy for the rails to support, however, and the company's board of directors decided not to take delivery of the other engines. The *Stourbridge Lion* was put to use as a stationary engine and was eventually scrapped. It was painted black and had wood, copper, and brass trimmings.

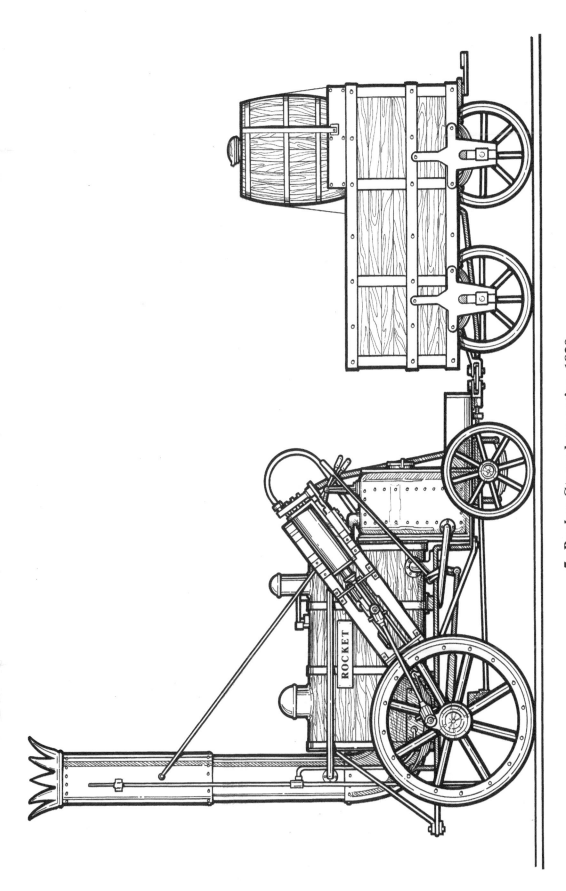

5. *Rocket.* Steam locomotive, 1829

One of the most significant events in railroad history occurred in October 1829 in the English countryside at Rainhill, near Liverpool. The Liverpool & Manchester Railway conducted a competition—known as the Rainhill Trials—to find the best locomotive design for its new railroad service. The rules specified that a locomotive weighing no more than 6 tons had to pull a load weighing 20 tons at an average speed of 10 mph. A prize of £500 was offered.

The only engine that successfully met the requirements was the *Rocket,* built by George Stephenson and his son Robert of the Robert Stephenson Company. Its boiler design was revolutionary, enabling it to produce greater power than any engine yet built. Pulling a 13-ton load, it averaged better than 12 mph over three days and at one point, running alone (without a load), reached a top speed of 29 mph—blistering for that era. The Stephensons won the prize and a contract to build eight more *Rocket*-type locomotives, which were put into regular service.

The *Rocket* is depicted pulling a car called a "tender" immediately behind it (all steam railroad engines pulled tenders to carry the fuel—wood, coal, or oil—and water needed to produce steam in their boilers). The *Rocket* had iron, copper, and brass fittings and was painted bright yellow with red trim.

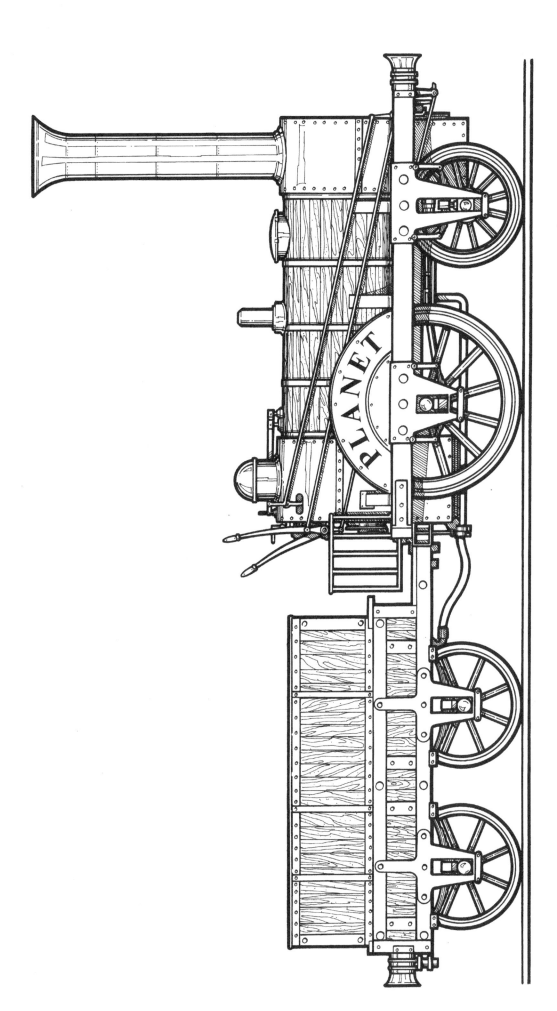

6. *Planet.* **Type 2-2-0 steam locomotive, 1830**

In 1830, the Stephenson Company designed for the Liverpool & Manchester Railway an important advance over earlier model locomotives. Called the *Planet*, this engine was the model for a succession of British and American locomotives produced over the next seventy-five years. It weighed about 12,000 pounds (the tender, with water and fuel, weighed about 8,000 pounds), and had a tractive effort of 1,450 pounds. Numerous *Planet*-type locomotives built by the company over the next few years were exported to Europe and the United States. The Stephensons went on to build an improved version of the *Planet* called the *Patentee*, which was also widely used on both continents. The *Patentee* had two additional wheels mounted on a third axle to improve stability.

As locomotives became more common and widespread in Europe and the U.S., a system was devised for their classification and identification, based on the number and position of their wheels. The first position/number represents the lead wheels, the next the driving wheels, and the last the trailing wheels. *The Planet* was a type 2-2-0 because it had two lead wheels, two driving wheels, and no trailing wheels. Its successor the *Patentee* was a type 2-2-2.

The *Planet* was painted black with green trim and had iron, copper, and brass fixtures.

7. *Best Friend of Charleston.* Steam locomotive, 1830

The first scheduled steam railway service in the United States began on Christmas Day, 1830. The locomotive *Best Friend of Charleston* pulled several cars carrying passengers over the six miles of track laid by the South Carolina Canal & Rail-Road Company. Eventually, the railroad constructed 136 miles of track between Charleston and Hamburg, S.C., over which it ran regular passenger and freight service.

The *Best Friend* was designed by Horatio Allen and built at the West Point Foundry in Cold Spring, New York, by Julius Petsch and Nicholas Darrell. It was driven by Allen on its first run. The engine was 14 feet long, weighed 6,000 pounds, and could reach a speed of 21 mph. It generated 6 hp and had a tractive effort of just 450 pounds. (In 1831, the foundry delivered to the railroad the *Best Friend's* twin, the *West Point*.)

Unfortunately, the *Best Friend* had a very short life. It exploded in 1831, killing the fireman when the steam exhaust valve was mistakenly tied shut. (A new locomotive, called the *Phoenix*, was built using its remains.) It was painted in the green, yellow, and red colors of the South Carolina Railroad.

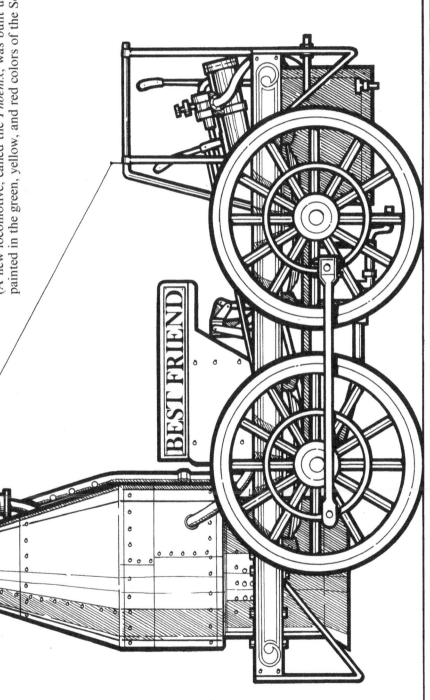

8. *Liverpool.* Type 2-2-0 steam locomotive, 1830

The *Liverpool* was designed by Edward Bury in 1830 and used on the Liverpool & Manchester Railway. Although smaller and less powerful than comparable *Planet*-type locomotives of the Stephenson Company, the *Liverpool* was reliable and less expensive. An interesting construction feature of all of Bury's engines was the bar frame, a structural element later incorporated into many nineteenth-century American-built locomotives. Bury's company, Bury, Curtis & Kennedy, built over four hundred "Bury engines" for several British railroads.

The *Liverpool* was twenty-six feet long, weighed 22,000 pounds, and had a tractive effort of 1,389 pounds. It carried 2,200 pounds of fuel and 400 gallons of water in its tender. The engine was painted in the green and black livery of the Liverpool & Manchester and had copper and brass fittings.

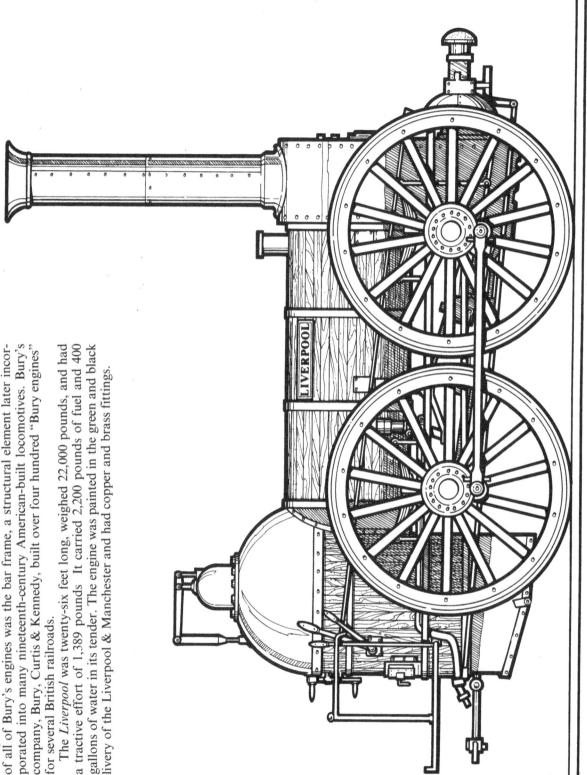

9. *DeWitt Clinton*. Steam locomotive, 1831

The first steam railway system in New York—and the second in the United States—began operation in 1831 with the railroad engine *DeWitt Clinton*, named after the governor responsible for the Erie Canal. The Mohawk & Hudson River Railroad Company built 16 miles of track for a route connecting the cities of Albany and Schenectady.

The *DeWitt Clinton* weighed about 5,000 pounds and could carry three to five carloads of coal at 30 mph. It transported freight and passengers in cars that resembled stagecoaches. It was designed by John B. Jervis and built at the West Point Foundry.

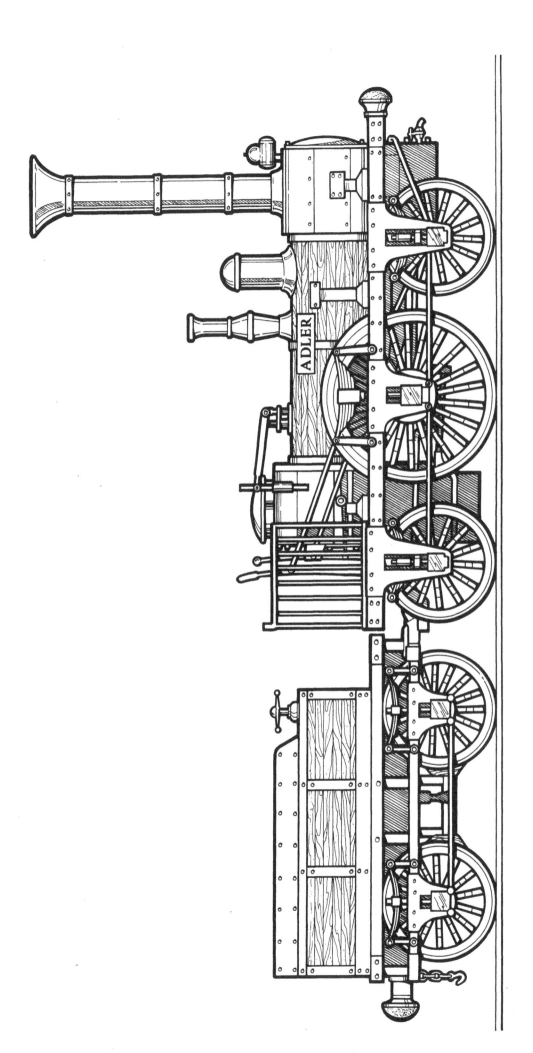

10. *Adler.* **Type 2-2-2 steam locomotive, 1835**

Germany began railroad service in 1835 with the introduction of the *Adler* ("Eagle") on the Nürnberg & Fürth Railway. The *Adler* was a *Patentee*-type 2-2-2 steam locomotive built in England by the Robert Stephenson Company. Shipped in parts and assembled in Nürnberg, it was 25 feet long, weighed 31,000 pounds, and had a tractive effort of 1,220 pounds. It remained in service on the Nürnberg & Fürth route, a distance of less than 4 miles, until 1857.

As railroad engines became more numerous, railway companies adopted specific colors and emblems to aid in public recognition and advertise their rail service. These distinctive colors became known as the companies' "livery" (by analogy with the distinctive costumes worn by the servants of nobility). The Nürnberg & Fürth Railway's livery was green, yellow, and red.

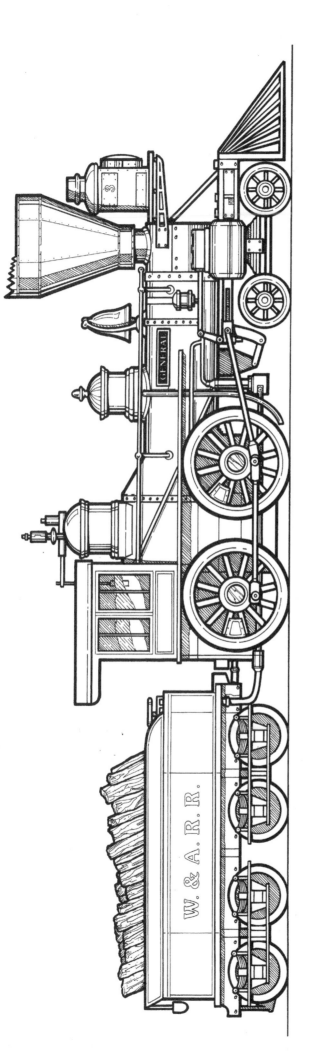

11. *General*. American class, type 4-4-0 steam locomotive, 1855

The classic American steam railroad engine of the mid-nineteenth century is typified by the *General*. It was designed by Thomas Rogers and built at the Rogers, Ketchum & Grosvenor works in Paterson, New Jersey, for the Western & Atlantic Railroad of Georgia in 1855. Most of its working life was spent running between Atlanta and Chattanooga, Tennessee. It was one of around 25,000 workhorse type 4-4-0 American class locomotives in operation by the time of the Civil War. Americans were among the most widely used and successful steam locomotives ever manufactured.

The *General* was involved in a famous Civil War incident in 1862. The locomotive and train were commandeered by a group of Union soldiers about 30 miles north of Atlanta to disrupt Confederate communications and supply lines. After eight hours and an 87-mile pursuit they were caught by Confederate forces, who executed them as spies. In recognition of their heroic efforts, Congress established the Medal of Honor, the highest American military award for valor.

The *General* was 52 feet long and weighed 90,000 pounds. The two cords of wood and 1,250 gallons of water in the tender allowed it to travel 50 miles before refueling. The engine had a tractive effort of 6,885 pounds and normally ran at 25 mph, but could reach 60 mph on a straight, level stretch of track. The *General* was painted in the black livery of the Western & Atlantic, and had bright copper and brass fittings.

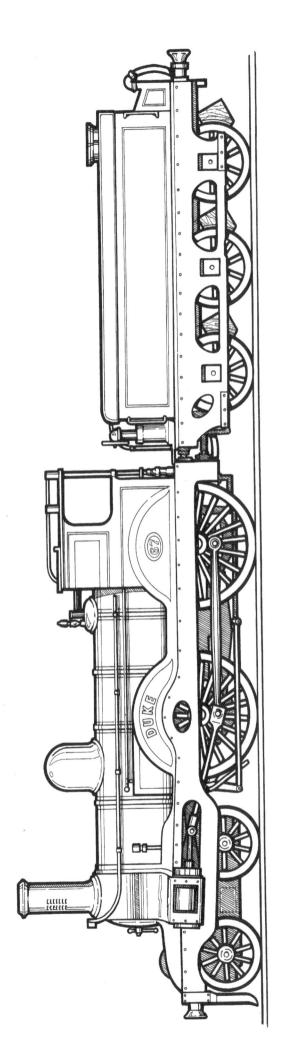

**12. Highland Railway Duke. American class,
type 4-4-0 steam locomotive, 1874**

The Duke class steam locomotive, a type 4-4-0 built by the Dubs Company of
Glasgow, was brought into service in 1874 by the Highland Railway of Scotland. It
was the most powerful railroad engine in use at the time; its considerable power was
needed to haul freight through the rugged Scottish highland terrain. These engines
had 12,338 pounds of tractive effort, were 51 feet long, and weighed 161,500 pounds.
The tenders carried 9,000 pounds of fuel and 1,800 gallons of water.

The last Duke locomotive was retired in 1923. No. 67, pictured above, was painted
in the yellow, red, and green livery of the Highland Railway.

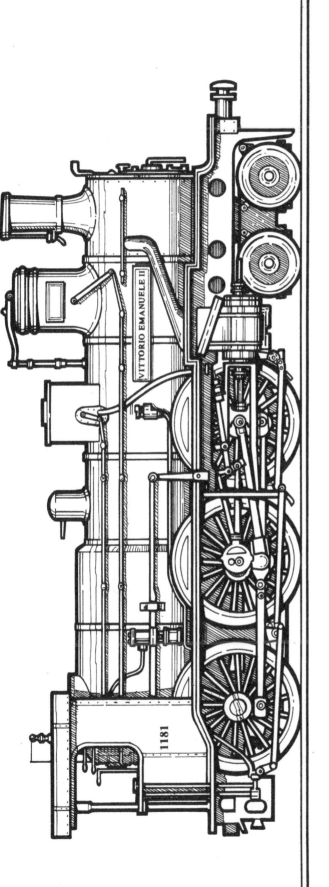

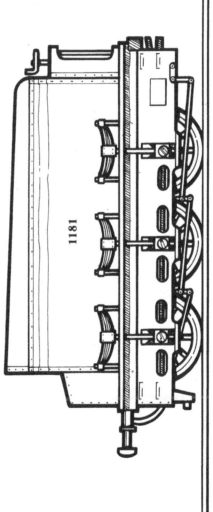

13. Upper Italy Railway Vittorio Emanuele II. Type 4-6-0 steam locomotive, 1884

The Vittorio Emanuele II was the first type 4-6-0 steam railroad engine to operate in Europe, entering service in 1884. It was designed to travel the route of the Upper Italy Railway connecting the industrial city of Turin, in the mountains, with the Ligurian seaport of Genoa. Its manufacture was a joint project of the Italian companies Ansaldo of Genoa and Miani & Sylvestri of Milan, and the German firm of Maffei.

A Vittorio Emanuele II could pull a 130-ton train of cars up the incline of the Apennine mountains at a steady speed of 25 mph. It was 54 feet long, weighed 184,474 pounds, and had a tractive effort of 15,335 pounds The tender was loaded with 7,700 pounds of fuel and 2,200 gallons of water. Vittorio Emanuele II steam locomotives were replaced by electric engines in 1910. The locomotive depicted above would have been painted in the green livery with black and yellow trim of the Upper Italy Railway.

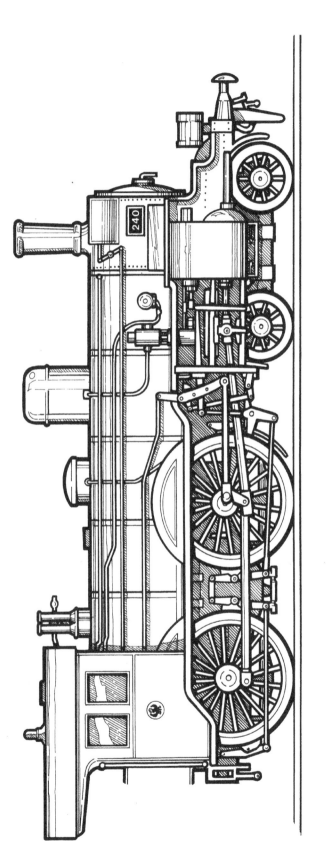

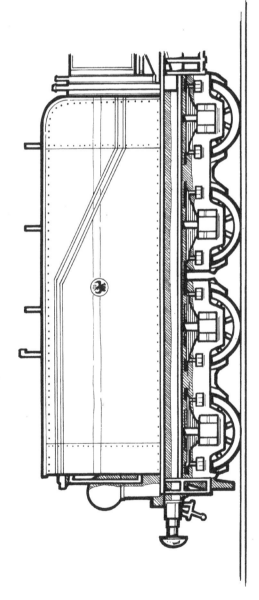

14. Prussian S-3. Type 4-4-0 steam locomotive, 1892

The most widely used railroad engine in Germany during the late nineteenth century was the powerful S-3, an American class (type 4-4-0) locomotive. Over a thousand were built between 1892 and 1904. The S-3 was the first steam locomotive to incorporate superheated steam into its boiler system to increase tractive effort. The engine generated a tractive effort of 18,500 pounds and could pull a 320-ton train at a steady 45 mph, or 150 tons on a 1 percent upgrade (one foot of vertical rise for every 100 feet of horizontal distance) at 30 mph. The S-3 was 57 feet long, weighed 112,000 pounds, and carried 11,000 pounds of fuel and 4,750 gallons of water in its tender.

The engine shown here was operated by the Royal Prussian Union Railway, and was painted in its colors of green, yellow, red, and black.

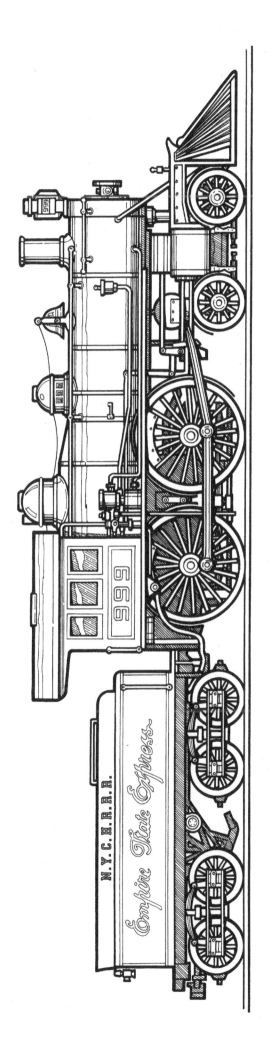

15. New York Central No. 999. American class, type 4-4-0 steam locomotive, 1893

American class (type 4-4-0) steam locomotives (sometimes called American Standards) were the most commonly used engines on American railroads from 1837 until after 1880, when the advent of air brakes allowed the use of longer and heavier trains, which in turn required more powerful locomotives. Some Americans remained in use, however, mostly on branch lines, until the 1950s.

An American became the fastest locomotive in the world on May 10, 1893, when it reached a speed of 112.5 mph on a straight stretch of track near Batavia, New York. The locomotive was the New York Central & Hudson Valley Railroad's No. 999, pulling the *Empire State Express*. The previous world record for locomo-

tive speed, 89.5 mph, was set by the London & North Eastern Railway's No. 604. On its record-setting run, No. 999 pulled four cars, each weighing 52 tons. The *Empire State Express* ran from New York City to Chicago during the Columbian Exposition of 1893, held in Chicago. It was the forerunner of the famous *Twentieth Century Limited* that the New York Central ran between the two cities for many years.

No. 999 was 57 feet long, weighed 204,000 pounds, and had a tractive effort of 16,270 pounds. As part of the *Empire State Express*, it was painted in black and gold.

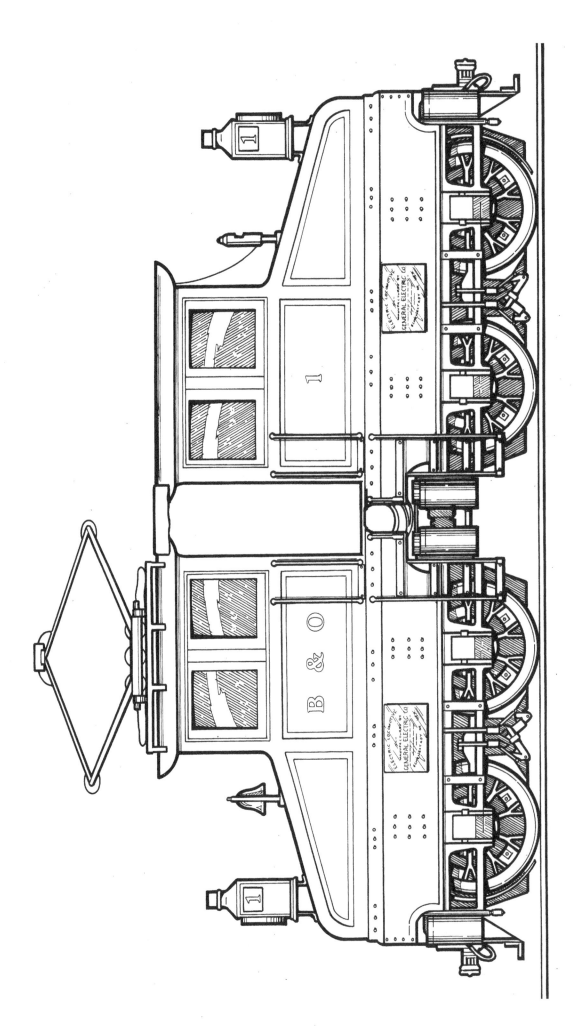

16. Baltimore & Ohio Electric Engine No. 1. Electric locomotive, 1895

The first electric-powered locomotive in regular service in the United States was the Baltimore & Ohio Railroad's Electric Engine No. 1. It was built in 1895 by the General Electric Company of Schenectady, New York. Actually a pair of motors coupled together, No. 1 was designed to pull trains—with their steam locomotives attached but not running—through the 1.4-mile-long Howard Street tunnel, where steam and smoke would have created hazardous conditions.

No. 1 and its companion units remained in regular service until 1912. No. 1 used direct current of 675 volts to power four electric motors of 360 hp each. Capable of up to 60 mph, it could haul freight trains of 1,200 tons through the tunnel at 15 mph. The engine was 27 feet long, weighed 192,000 pounds, and had a considerable tractive effort of 45,000 pounds. It was painted in the olive green and yellow livery of the B&O.

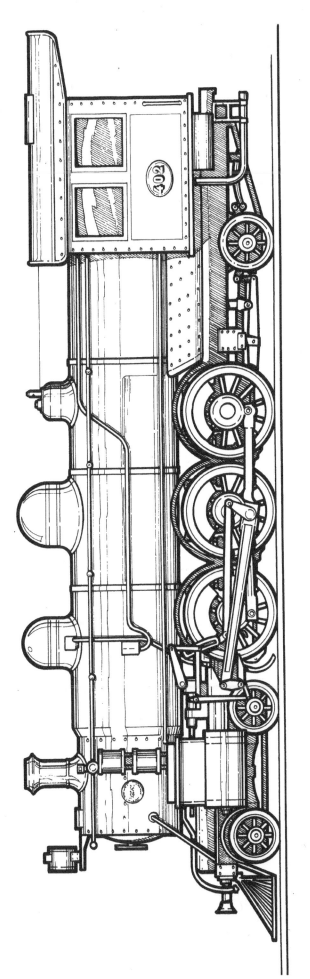

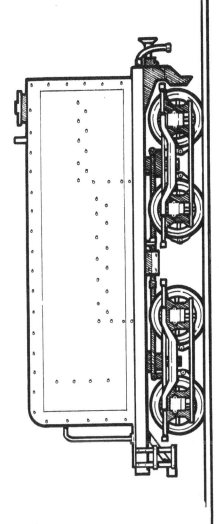

17. New Zealand Government Railways Q. Pacific class, type 4-6-2 steam locomotive, 1901

One of the most versatile and widely-used steam railroad engines of the early twentieth century was the Pacific class locomotive, type 4-6-2. Heavier and more powerful than the American class, it became, in many design variations, the standard passenger locomotive until the advent of diesels. Eventually more than 6,000 were operated by American railroads.

Although locomotives with a 4-6-2 configuration had been built before, it is considered that the first real Pacific class engines were those made by the Baldwin Locomotive Works of Philadelphia for the New Zealand Government Railways (which designated them its Q class). From 1901 to 1956, a total of 343 of these rugged and reliable machines were in operational service.

The New Zealand Q, which was smaller than later American Pacifics, was 55 feet long, weighed 165,000 pounds, and produced a tractive effort of 19,540 pounds. The tender carried 11,000 pounds of fuel and 1,700 gallons of water. The engine shown was painted in the NZGR's colors of black and gold.

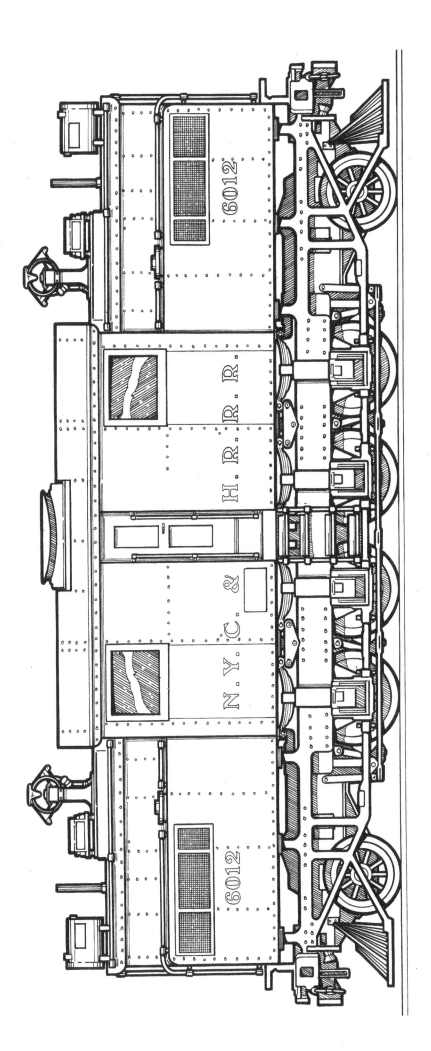

18. New York Central S. Electric locomotive, 1906

The New York Central & Hudson River Railroad began testing electric engines in 1904. Regular operations began in 1906 with the S class on the line between Harmon, north of New York City, and Grand Central Terminal. (A fatal accident in 1902 in the tunnel leading to Grand Central had led the New York State legislature to ban the use of steam locomotives in Manhattan.)

The S, designed primarily by Asa F. Batchelder of General Electric and built by the American Locomotive Company (ALCO) and GE, was powered by four electric motors, each rated at 550 hp, that were fed 660 volts of direct current from a track-mounted third rail. It was also equipped with two pantographs (folding frameworks mounted atop the engine) to draw power from overhead lines, called catenary cables, in places where a third rail was thought to be impractical. A total of forty-six S class electrics were put into service, one of which remained in use until 1961. The S could pull 450 tons at a steady 60 mph with its tractive effort of 32,000 pounds. It was 37 feet long and weighed 200,500 pounds. These engines were painted in the black and white colors of the New York Central.

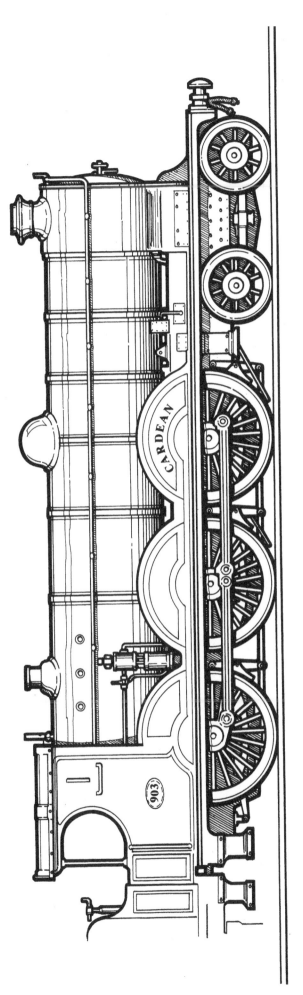

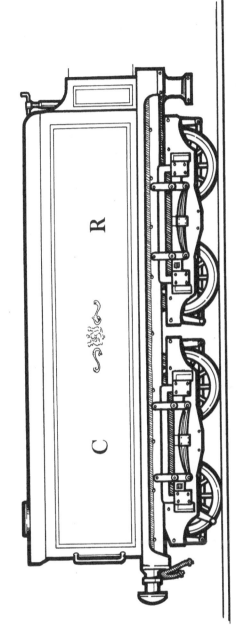

19. Caledonian CL8 Cardean. Type 4-6-0 steam locomotive, 1906

The Caledonian Railway's Cardean railroad engine, a type 4-6-0, is a fine example of the engines of the golden age of steam rail transport. For power, reliability, and graceful appearance, this machine had few rivals. The Cardean, designated by the railway the CL8, was the creation of famed locomotive designer John Farquharson Macintosh. It was built by the Caledonian in 1906 at its own works in St. Rollox, Scotland.

The Cardean was 65 feet long, weighed 294,000 pounds, and produced 22,667 pounds of tractive effort. The tender carried 11,000 pounds of fuel and 5,000 gallons of water. The Caledonian Railway dressed its engines in livery of "Caledonian" blue with black and gold trim. The last of this class of steam locomotive was retired in 1930.

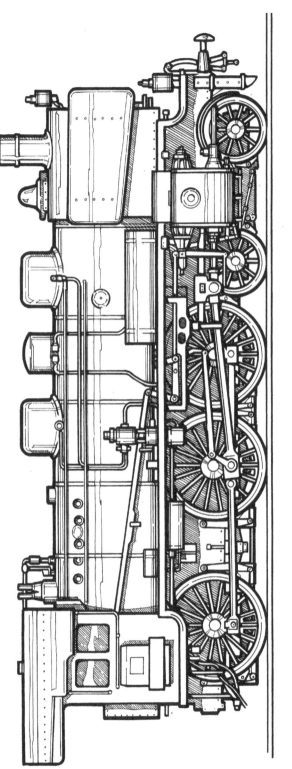

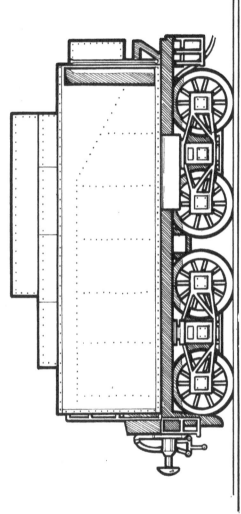

20. Prussian P-8. Type 4-6-0 steam locomotive, 1906

The most successful and widely used railroad engines in Europe during the early years of the twentieth century were those of the German P-8 class, built initially for the Royal Prussian Union Railway in 1906. From 1906 to 1928, a total of 3,438 P-8s were manufactured in Germany, and another 500 were built under license in other European countries.

Used for both passenger and freight operations, P-8s could transport 700 tons on a level track at a constant 50 mph, and handle a 1 percent upgrade with 300 tons while maintaining 30 mph. The engine was 61 feet long, weighed 172,500 pounds, and had 27,760 pounds of tractive effort, giving it a top speed of 68 mph. The last P-8 used in Germany was retired in 1966, while in other parts of Europe they continued operating until 1979, giving this machine an incredible seventy-three-year service life. The P-8 shown here wore colors of the German Federal Railway—medium green with red trim.

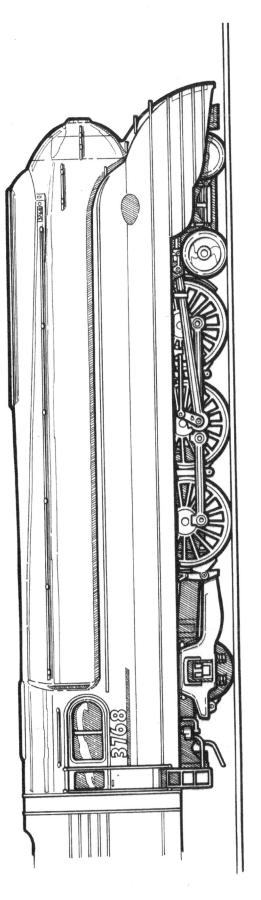

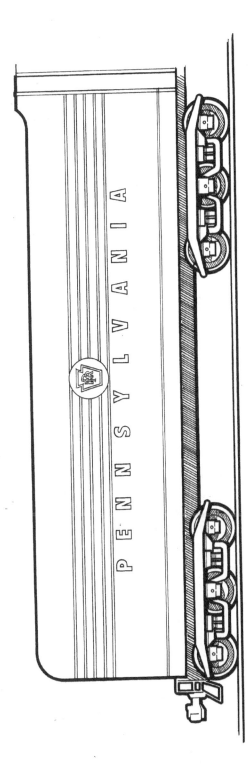

21. Pennsylvania K-4. Pacific class, type 4-6-2 steam locomotive, 1914

The Pennsylvania Railroad, which thought of itself as the benchmark against which other railroads should be measured, had extremely high standards of service and adherence to schedules. It created a classic and very reliable steam railroad engine in 1914, the K-4 Pacific. From 1914 to 1928, the company built 425 K-4s at its own workshops in Altoona, Pennsylvania. The famous *Broadway Limited* between New York City's Penn Station and Chicago was pulled by mighty K-4 locomotives during the 1920s and '30s.

The K-4 depicted is a fully streamlined version whose outer body paneling was designed in 1935 by one of the leading industrial designers of the period, Raymond Loewy. His approach to locomotive styling was elegant and distinctive. Loewy created several other memorable streamlined engine styles for the "Pennsy," including the GG-1 electric and the S-1 and T-1 steam locomotives. Unfortunately, the K-4's streamlined body panels proved impractical, making access for maintenance difficult. The panels were later modified and ultimately removed.

The K-4 was 83 feet long, weighed 309,000 pounds, and had a tractive effort of 44,460 pounds. The tenders were built in several types, carrying from 25,000 to 63,000 pounds of coal and from 7,000 to 22,000 gallons of water. The K-4 shown here was painted in the black and gold livery of the Pennsylvania Railroad.

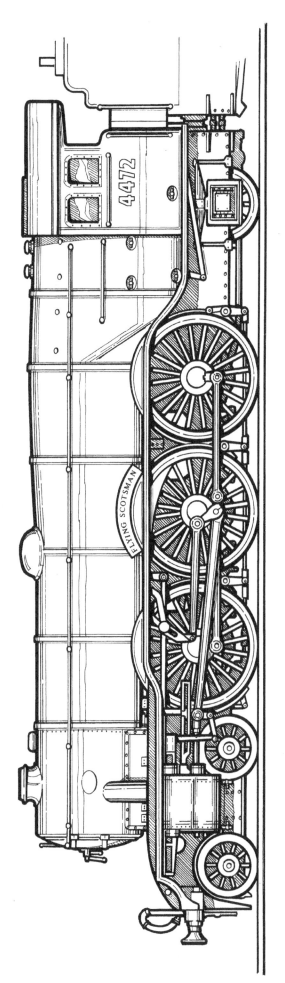

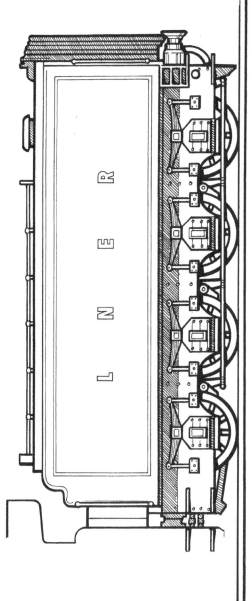

22. London & North Eastern A1 *Flying Scotsman.* Pacific class, type 4-6-2 steam locomotive, 1922

The *Flying Scotsman* is a passenger express train that has been operated since 1862 between London and Edinburgh by the Great Northern Railway and its successor companies. Of the many locomotives used on this train over the years, the most famous were probably the Pacific class engines created by famed engineer Sir Nigel Gresley. Between 1922 and 1934, 110 of these engines were built at the railroad's own Doncaster Works. Those built in 1922–34 were designated A1s and A3s; the 1935–38 models, which were streamlined, were designated A4s (see Plate 25).

The original model A1 was 64 feet long, weighed 200,000 pounds, and produced 29,385 pounds of tractive effort. The tender carried 18,000 pounds of fuel and 5,000 gallons of water. The sole surviving member of this class, Engine No. 4472, named *The Flying Scotsman,* is shown here. It was the first new locomotive delivered to the newly formed London & North Eastern Railway in early 1923, and was given its name in 1924. It was later rebuilt as an A3 and was retired from regular operation in 1963. It is shown painted in the green and black livery of the London & North Eastern Railway.

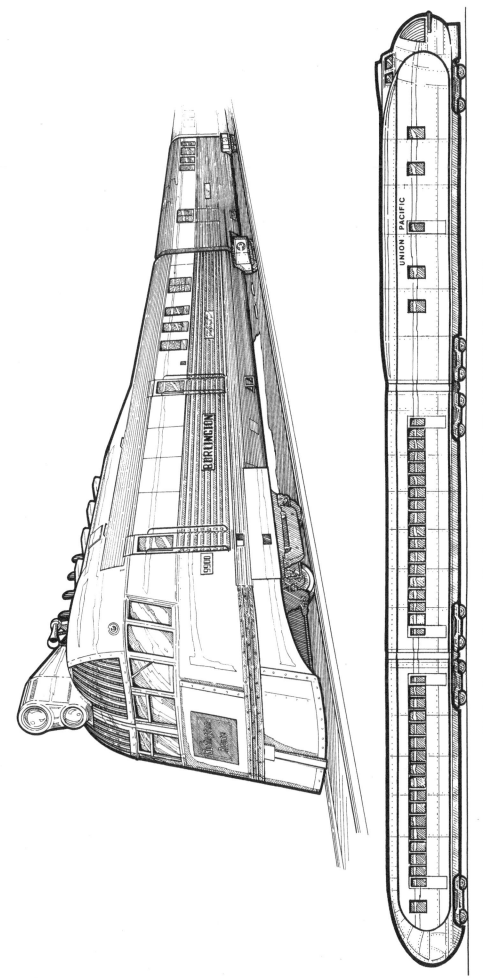

23. Burlington *Pioneer Zephyr* and Union Pacific M-10000 *City of Salina*.
Diesel-electric locomotives, 1934

In 1934, two railroad companies were in tight competition to introduce the first diesel-electric engine into regular service. It was a very close race. The Union Pacific Railroad was the technical winner with its M-10000 three-car trainset in February of 1934 (a trainset is comprised of cars permanently hooked together). However, due to development problems, it ran with a petroleum distillate engine (similar to a gasoline engine).

The Chicago, Burlington & Quincy Railroad, known as the Burlington Route, introduced its *Zephyr* stainless steel three-car trainset, powered by a General Motors diesel engine, in May 1934. In November, Union Pacific introduced a modified six-car version of the M-10000, designated the M-10001, with true diesel power.

Although the M-10000 was first into service, the *Zephyr* engine was the true winner owing to its enormous success and popularity with the public. The M-10000 later went into regular service as the *City of Salina* between Kansas City and Salina, Kansas. It carried 116 passengers in three air-conditioned cars and could hit 90 mph.

The *Zephyr* quickly established a new record for the Chicago-to-Denver run with an average speed of almost 78 mph. It later went into regular service between Kansas City and Lincoln, Nebraska. The three-car trainset was 196 feet long, weighed 175,000 pounds, and could reach speeds of 110 mph. It attracted huge crowds of people along its route who were eager to see the sleek, shiny stainless-steel streamliner. The original seventy-two-seat *Zephyr* (renamed the *Pioneer Zephyr* when the Burlington gave "Zephyr" names to its other express trains) ran over three million miles and is now on permanent exhibit at the Chicago Museum of Science and Industry, completely restored to its original condition.

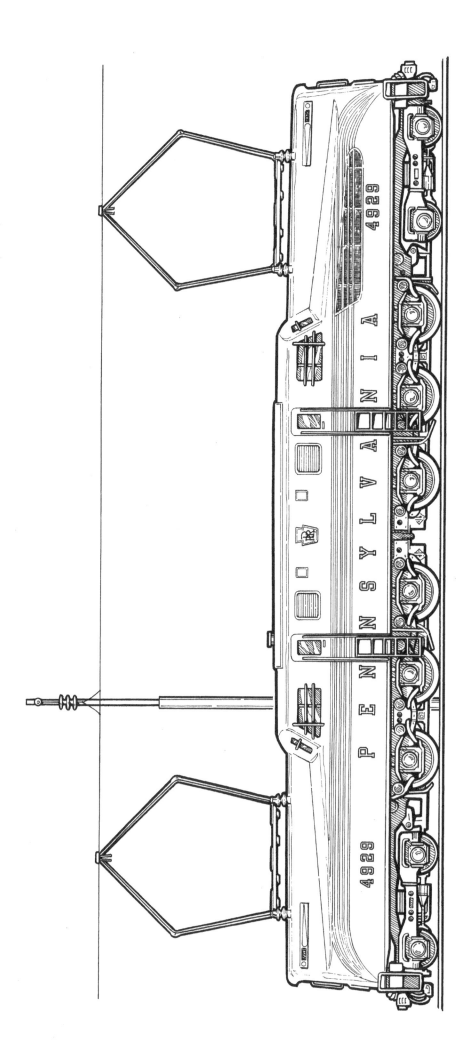

24. Pennsylvania GG-1. Electric locomotive, 1934

The Pennsylvania Railroad's GG-1 locomotive was a powerful, versatile, and rugged electric railroad engine. It was powered by twelve electric motors, each generating 410 hp, for a combined total of 4,920 hp and 70,000 pounds of tractive effort. The engine drew power from 15,000-volt overhead power lines through a pantograph. The GG-1 regularly pulled twenty passenger cars at speeds of up to 90 mph.

The streamlined body of the GG-1 was a very smooth, welded, one-piece unit that was lowered onto the frame in a single piece during construction. Other railroad engines designed or modified for streamlining had individual body panels riveted into position. The GG-1 was a another Raymond Loewy design for the Pennsylvania.

The GG-1s were built in the Pennsy's own Altoona workshops as well as at the Baldwin Locomotive Works in Philadelphia. Their electrical equipment was manufactured by General Electric and Westinghouse. A total of 139 of these powerful workhorse electrics were built between 1935 and 1943; some remained in service in the 1980s. They were 79 feet long and weighed 477,000 pounds. The one shown here, a GG-1A, was painted either black, green, or red, with gold pinstripes and lettering.

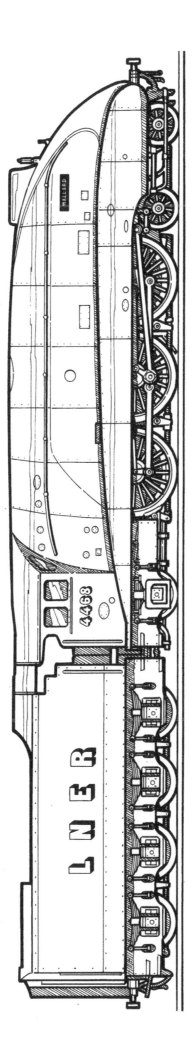

25. London & North Eastern A4 *Mallard*. Pacific class, type 4-6-2 steam locomotive, 1935

The world record for the fastest steam locomotive ever operated in regular service belongs to a London & North Eastern Railway A4 locomotive named the *Mallard*. The A4 was a Pacific class engine designed by the British railroad engineer Sir Nigel Gresley for the LNER. On July 4, 1938, the *Mallard* established the record with a sustained speed of 126 mph. On one run between London and Newcastle, the *Mallard* maintained a steady speed of 100 mph for a distance of twenty-five miles.

Thirty-one A4 Pacifics were built for the LNER between 1935 and 1938. The A4 was 71 feet long and weighed 206,000 pounds, relatively light for its powerful tractive effort of 35,455 pounds. The tender was completely streamlined into the engine and carried 18,000 pounds of fuel and 6,000 gallons of water. Engine No. 4468, the *Mallard*, was painted in the royal blue and dark blue livery of the London & North Eastern Railway.

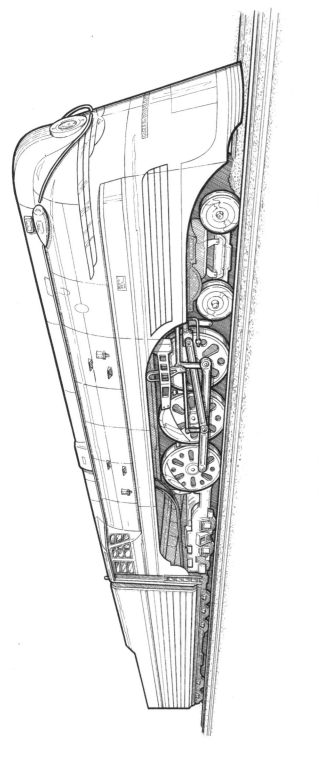

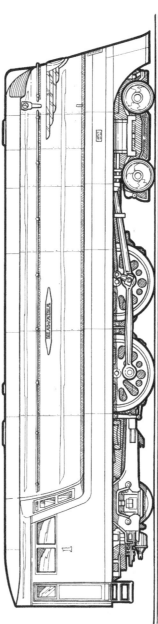

26. Milwaukee A, Atlantic class, type 4-4-2 steam locomotive, 1935. Milwaukee F7, Hudson class, type 4-6-4 steam locomotive, 1938

The first steam locomotives specifically designed to cruise at 100 mph were built by the American Locomotive Company (ALCO) for the Chicago, Milwaukee, St. Paul & Pacific Railroad, known as the Milwaukee Road. These were the Milwaukee's Atlantic class As and Hudson class F7s. Both engines were classic examples of streamlining for both function and eye-appeal.

The first into service were the As in 1935. They were rated at 3,000 hp and 30,376 pounds of tractive effort, and ran on oil rather than coal. Four were built. They were intended as passenger train locomotives, and were used primarily on the six-car *Hiawatha* express train between Chicago and Minneapolis/St. Paul, propelling it at speeds of up to 110 mph. They were the last type 4-4-2 locomotives ever built. In 1938, the larger F7s, which succeeded previous freight engines in the Milwaukee's F series (built by the Baldwin Locomotive Works), were put

into service on the *Hiawatha* as well as on heavy freight trains. Six were built. The F7s could reach 120 mph while pulling a 55-ton twelve-car train. They were 100 feet long, weighed 415,000 pounds with tender, and produced 50,295 pounds of tractive effort. The tenders held 45,000 pounds of coal and 16,700 gallons of water.

Diesel-engine locomotives gradually replaced these graceful steam-driven Atlantics and Hudsons on the Milwaukee Road beginning in 1941. By 1951 they had all been retired. During their years of operation they were the fastest steam locomotives in regular service and represented a high point in streamlined locomotive design. They were painted in the Milwaukee Road's colors of yellow with orange, maroon, and brown trim.

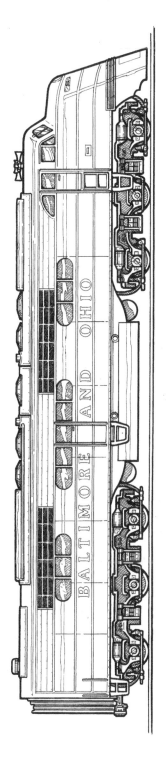

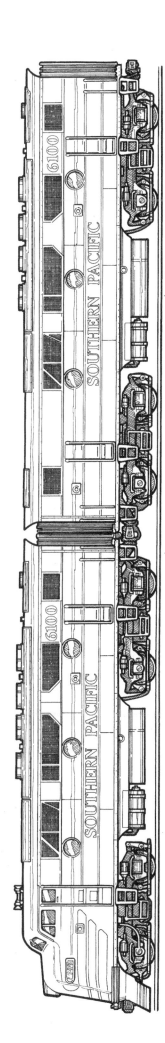

27. General Motors E and F. Diesel-electric locomotives, 1937/1939

With the introduction, widespread use, and great success of these two streamlined diesel-electric railroad engines, the hundred-year reign of the steam locomotive was effectively ended. The E and F series were built by the Electro-Motive Division (EMD) of General Motors Corporation. They were fast, powerful, reliable, and could be coupled into dual or triple units for extra power.

The first to enter service, in 1937, was the E series streamlined passenger engine. Shown above is the cab or A unit, which could be coupled to a B or booster unit for additional horsepower (the booster units lack only the forward crew cabin). The cab unit was 71 feet long and weighed 212,310 pounds; the booster was 70 feet and weighed 205,000 pounds. Each unit's two diesel engines produced 1,800 hp and 53,080 pounds of tractive effort. The E series engine depicted was painted in the dark blue, silver, and white livery of the Baltimore & Ohio Railroad.

The F series, also built in cab and booster units, was introduced in 1939 and was intended for both freight and passenger service. The earliest (FT) units were 50 feet long, weighed over 230,000 pounds, and had 57,500 pounds of tractive force created by their 1,350 hp diesels. The F series A and B units shown wore the black with silver and red trim of the Southern Pacific Railroad.

Extremely reliable and much easier to maintain than steam locomotives, the E and F series set many railroad records. One E series engine ran for 365 consecutive days without a mechanical breakdown. A total of 2,495 E and F series engines in various models, including cabs and boosters, were built between 1937 and 1960. Many are still in use with railroads around the world.

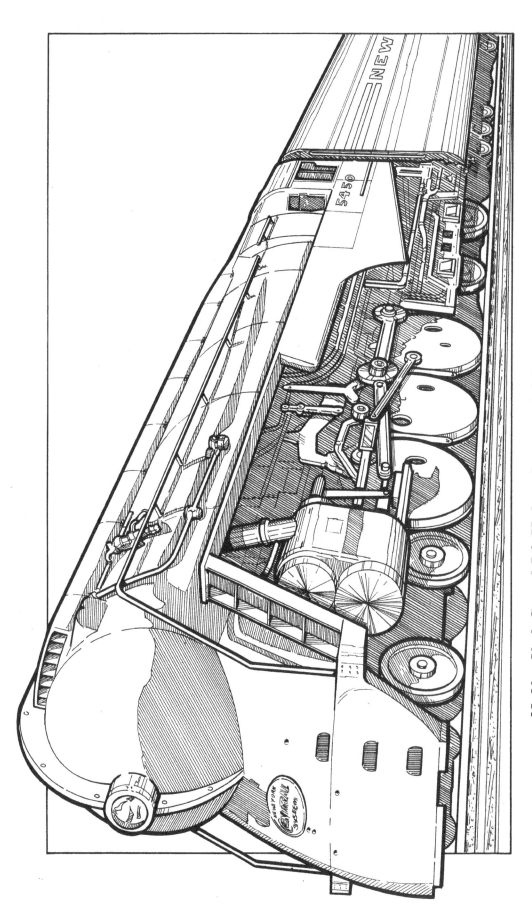

28. New York Central J-3. Hudson class, type 4-6-4 steam locomotive, 1937

Another very successful steam locomotive was the J-3, a Hudson class (type 4-6-4) locomotive operated by the New York Central Railroad, the great rival to the Pennsylvania. The Hudsons were developed and built for the New York Central by the American Locomotive Company (ALCO), and took their name from the Central's Hudson River route. There were three J class models; the powerful J-3 of 1938 succeeded the J-1 and J-2, introduced in 1927. The final ten J-3s produced were given streamlined body panels created by industrial designer Henry Dreyfuss. These were used on the famous *Twentieth Century Limited* passenger express that ran between New York and Chicago. With its bold crested helmet nose, the New York Central J-3 streamliner became one of the most recognizable and dramatic images of the streamline design movement of the 1930s and '40s. The streamlined paneling was removed after 1945.

The J-3s could travel at 60 mph while pulling a train weighing 1,650 tons. They were 96 feet long, weighed 365,000 pounds (665,000 with tender), and developed 43,440 pounds of tractive effort. Their tenders carried a mighty load of 56,000 pounds of coal and 14,000 gallons of water. At the end of World War II, most were still in service, but would soon be replaced by the newer technology of diesel-electric railroad engines. The streamlined J-3 shown here was painted in the New York Central's black, silver, and white livery.

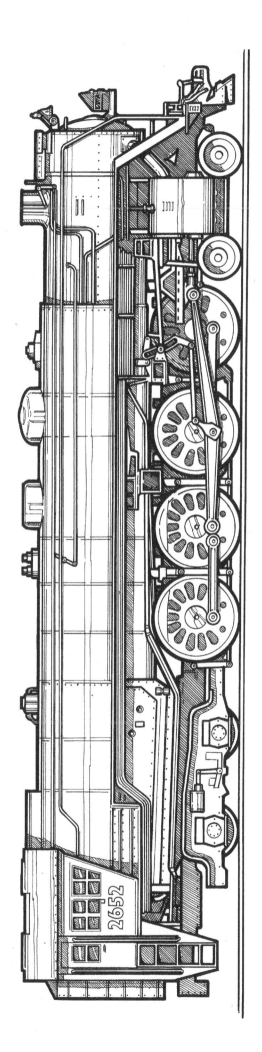

29. Northern Pacific A-4 and A-5. Northern class, type 4-8-4 steam locomotives, 1941/1943

Some of the earliest steam locomotives with eight driving wheels were the type 4-8-4 Northerns built for the Northern Pacific Railroad, from which the class took its name. The first, designated by Northern Pacific its A class, was introduced in 1926. It was built by the American Locomotive Company (ALCO) to haul heavy freight on the North Coast Route from St. Paul, Minnesota, to Livingston, Montana—a distance of 999 miles.

The A-4, introduced in 1941, was built by the Baldwin Locomotive Works.

It was 109 feet long, weighed 492,800 pounds (with tender, 878,850), and had a tractive effort of 69,800 pounds. The tender held 54,000 pounds of coal and 20,000 gallons of water. An upgraded version, the A-5, was introduced in 1943. It was built by Baldwin and was basically identical to the A-4 except that it was heavier at 508,500 pounds. These engines would have been painted in the black, gray, and white livery of the Northern Pacific Railroad.

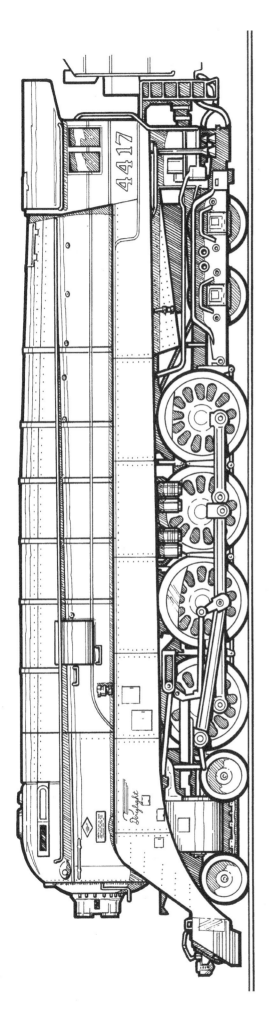

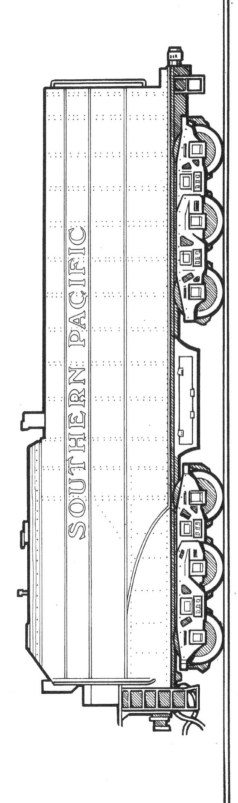

30. Southern Pacific Golden States GS-4. Northern class, type 4-8-4 steam locomotive, 1941

Many railroad enthusiasts consider the Southern Pacific Railroad's GS-4 locomotive to be the finest example of a streamlined steam railroad engine. Although not fully enclosed in drag-reducing body panels, the GS-4 combined the inherent visual excitement of the steam locomotive's display of drive wheels, connecting rods, and other running gear, with the eye-appeal, speed, and fuel economy of streamlining.

The Southern Pacific's Golden States locomotives (the SP preferred not to use the designation "Northern" since it derived from the name of a rival railroad) were used to haul the famous *Daylight* coast line passenger express train between Los Angeles and San Francisco, a distance of 470 miles. The first of the GS series, the GS-1s, were built by the Baldwin Locomotive Works in 1930. Later models were built by the Lima Locomotive Works of Lima, Ohio. Twenty-eight GS-4s were delivered in 1941 and 1942. The GS-4 could pull a train weighing 586 tons at speeds reaching 95 mph. It was fueled with oil rather than the more commonly used coal.

The GS-4 was 101 feet long, weighed 475,000 pounds (865,750 with tender), and had a mighty tractive effort of 64,800 pounds. The twelve-wheeled tender held 5,900 gallons of oil and 23,300 gallons of water. No. 4417, the engine depicted here, was painted in Southern Pacific's special Daylight livery of black, gray, red, and orange.

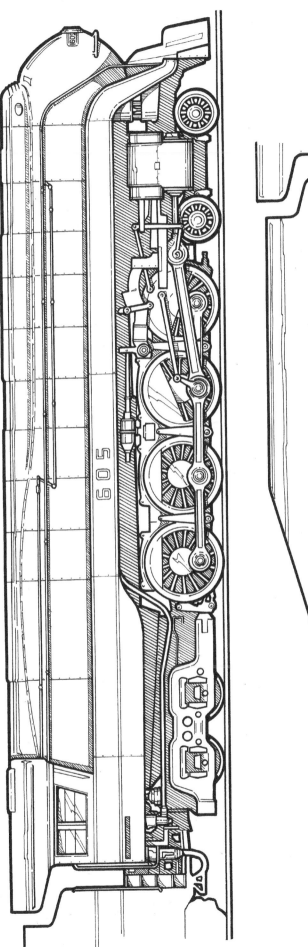

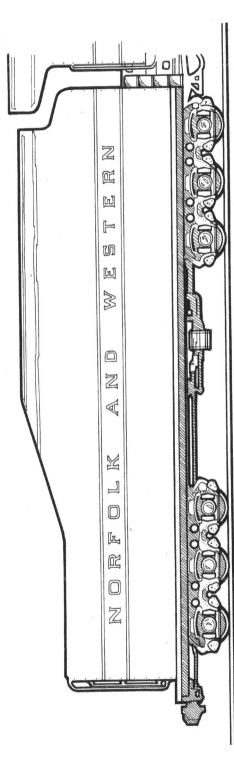

31. Norfolk & Western J. Northern class, type 4-8-4 steam locomotive, 1941

A rugged and powerful example of a type 4-8-4 steam railroad engine was the Norfolk & Western Railroad's J class, pictured above with its streamlined shrouding. Designed and built at the Norfolk's own Roanoke shops, the engine could run at 90 mph while pulling a train of 1,000 tons. It was introduced in 1941 and was used to pull the *Powhatan Arrow* and other passenger express trains between Cincinnati and Norfolk, Virginia. The last one was retired in 1961. It was the last American steam locomotive in regular service.

The Norfolk's J engine was 109 feet long, weighed 494,000 pounds (873,000 with tender), and produced a tremendous 80,000 pounds of tractive effort with an estimated 5,000 hp. This power was needed to haul freight and passengers through the rugged Appalachian Mountains. The tender, which blended smoothly into the streamlined locomotive body, carried 70,000 pounds of coal and 20,000 gallons of water. The livery of the Norfolk & Western was black with broad red stripes and yellow accent stripes.

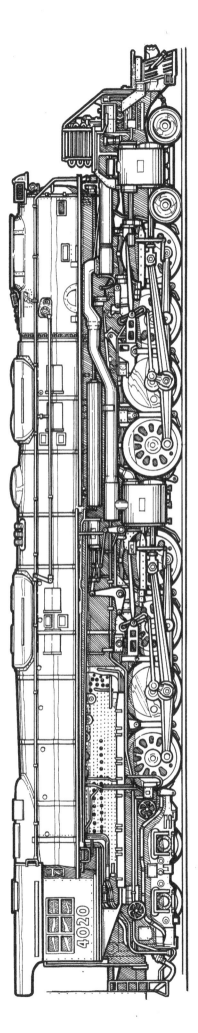

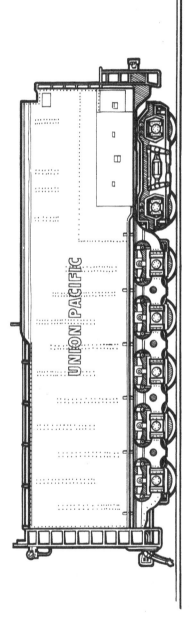

32. Union Pacific Big Boy. Type 4-8-8-4 steam locomotive, 1941

The largest and most powerful steam railroad engine ever used in regular service was the type 4-8-8-4 Big Boy operated by the Union Pacific Railroad starting in 1942. This behemoth, built by the American Locomotive Company, was designed to haul 3,000 tons of freight up the incline of the Wasatch Mountains of Utah and Wyoming and over the Continental Divide. By any measurement, the Big Boy was a giant among railroad engines. With its double set of eight driving wheels, it stretched 93 feet (132 feet with tender) and weighed 762,000 pounds (an immense 1.2 million pounds with fully loaded tender). The Big Boy was articulated, meaning that the two sets of eight driving wheels were connected by a pivoting hinge frame, allowing the enormously long engine to bend around curves in the track.

The steam boiler produced an estimated 6,300 hp and developed a record-setting 137,500 pounds of tractive effort. Fueling this mighty engine required 24,000 pounds of coal and 12,500 gallons of water every hour. Big Boys were as reliable as they were powerful; one, No. 4019, was in regular service from 1942 to 1961, completing 1,043,532 miles of travel. Twenty-five Big Boys were produced for the Union Pacific, which painted them in its light and dark gray livery

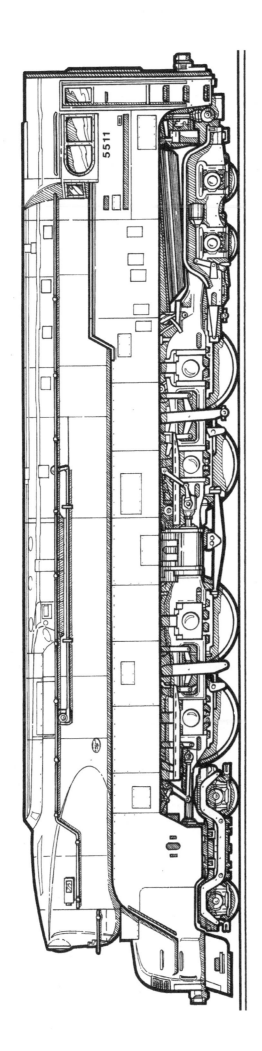

33. Pennsylvania T-1. Type 4-4-4-4 duplex steam locomotive, 1942

One of the most distinctive-looking and complex steam railroad engines ever built was the Pennsylvania Railroad's type 4-4-4-4 T-1 duplex. "Duplex" refers to the drive system, which was arranged in two sets of cylinders and pistons, each moving two sets of four drive wheels. The T-1's unique streamlined body was designed by Raymond Loewy.

The T-1 was primarily a fast passenger locomotive designed to pull 880-ton trains at 100 mph between Harrisburg and Chicago. Fifty-two T-1s were built between 1942 and 1946 at the Pennsy's Altoona workshops and at the Baldwin Locomotive Works.

The T-1 was 122 feet long with tender, weighed 945,000 pounds, and had an estimated 6,500 hp producing 64,700 pounds of tractive effort. The tender carried 85,000 pounds of fuel and 16,700 gallons of water. The T-1s were retired by 1949 owing to the too-frequent maintenance requirements of their complicated duplex drive system. The T-1 pictured was painted in the PRR's light gray and gold livery.

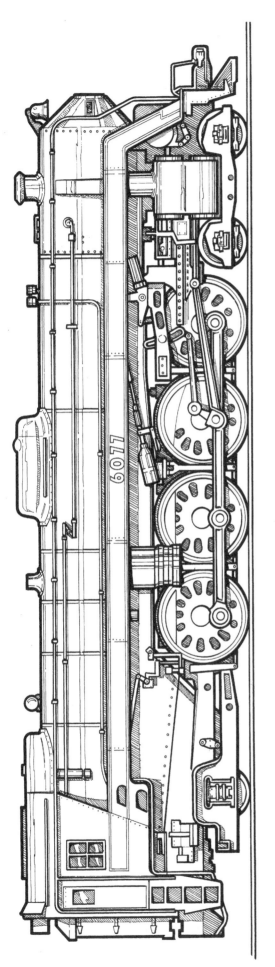

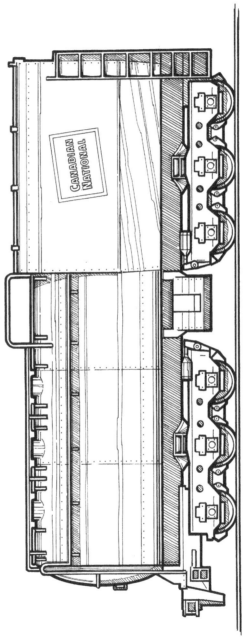

34. Canadian National U1-f. Mountain class, type 4-8-2 steam locomotive, 1944

The Mountain class locomotive, type 4-8-2, was first developed for the Chesapeake & Ohio Railroad in 1911, to haul ever larger trains over the Allegheny Mountains without having to double up its locomotives to generate sufficient power. North American railroads eventually bought over 2,200 Mountains between 1911 and 1946.

The Canadian National Railways, formed in 1923, ordered its first Mountain class locomotive the same year. These were designated U1-as. Subsequent models of the U class were delivered throught the 1920s.

The last Mountains ordered by the CNR were twenty U1-fs, built by the

Montreal Locomotive Works and brought into service in 1944. These sturdy and powerful engines were employed by the CNR to bridge the continent. On regular cross-country runs, U1-fs could pull 700 tons while traveling at 80 mph. The U1-f, with its unusual cylindrical tender, was 93 feet long, weighed 416,500 pounds (638,000 with tender), and generated 52,500 pounds of tractive effort. The tender carried 36,000 pounds of coal and 14,375 gallons of water. The U1-f depicted was painted in the bright green with black-and-red-accented livery of the Canadian National Railways.

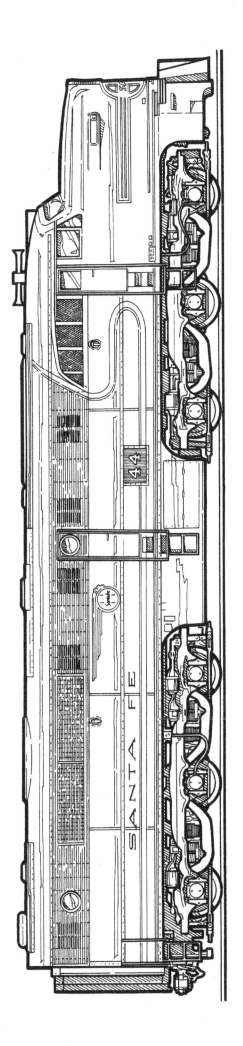

35. ALCO PA. Diesel-electric locomotives, 1946

The American Locomotive Company (ALCO) had a long history of building powerful and reliable railroad engines. Its designs include such illustrious machines as the early American class locomotives, the New York Central J-3 Hudsons, the Milwaukee Road A Atlantics and F7 Hudsons, and the Union Pacific Big Boys. Beginning in 1946, it introduced the first in a series of diesel-electric locomotives that were operated for more than thirty years by most of the major railroads. The passenger version was designated the P series. The PA cab units could be combined with the PB booster units to create multiple-engined powerhouses capable of pulling the longest trains.

ALCO also introduced the F series, engines designed for fast freight hauling,

consisting of the FA (cab) and FB (booster) units. The P and F series were the last significant locomotives to be manufactured by ALCO. A total of 1,282 P and F model locomotives were built before ALCO ceased operations in 1969—part of the general decline of the railroad industry.

The PA cab unit depicted here was 65 feet long and weighed 306,000 pounds. Its 2,000-hp diesel engine provided the PA with 33,000 pounds of tractive effort. It had a top speed of 117 mph. It was painted in the memorable livery of the Atchison, Topeka, and Santa Fe Railroad's *Super Chief* that ran between Chicago and Los Angeles for many years. The Santa Fe's colors are red, yellow, and black against the unpainted silver aluminum body panels.

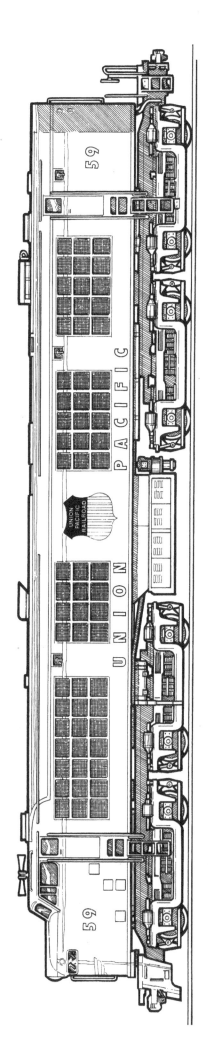

36. Union Pacific GTEL. Gas turbine-electric locomotive, 1952

In keeping with the Union Pacific tradition of operating large and powerful single-unit railroad engines (like the Big Boys), the company introduced a gas turbine-electric engine model in 1952, after having tested one thoroughly in 1949. Turbine engines, in development since the 1930s, were an offshoot of the same technology that had produced the jet engine. The advantage of a gas turbine is its very high power-to-weight ratio. The first Union Pacific gas turbine, built by ALCO and General Electric, developed 4,500 hp, which translated into a tremendous tractive effort of 135,000 pounds, slightly less than the mighty Big Boy. These impressive machines were built by GE in three groups, generating pro-

gressively greater horsepower. The last thirty engines, delivered in 1958–61, were rated at 8,500 hp. Union Pacific operated a total of fifty-five gas turbine engines from 1949 to 1969. Unfortunately, their fuel consumption was enormous—so enormous that they had to have tenders attached to carry additional fuel, like steam engines. Cooling the turbine blades proved to be an insuperable problem, and they made so much noise they could not be operated in heavily populated areas. They were eventually replaced by smaller, less expensive, and easier-to-maintain diesel-electric engines. No. 59, shown above, appeared in the yellow, red, and black livery of the Union Pacific Railroad.

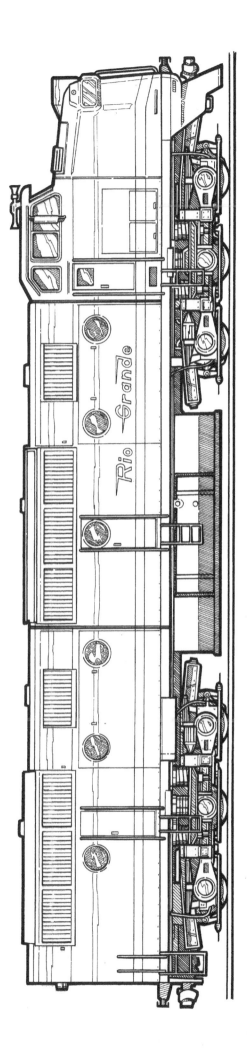

37. Krauss–Maffei ML4000. Diesel-electric locomotive, 1961

The Denver & Rio Grande Western Railroad made an unusual move in 1961 by purchasing six of these German-made diesel-electric locomotives. They were distinctive in being the only foreign-built railroad engines to enter service in the U.S. since the early nineteenth century. The Rio Grande was initially attracted to the Krauss-Maffei model by virtue of its sophisticated and efficient transmission system, an advance over other systems in general use at the time. In 1963, the Southern Pacific Railroad, which had taken over the Rio Grande's routes, ordered fifteen new Krauss-Maffei engines. These locomotives were often coupled in teams of two or three for a total of 8,000 to 12,000 hp. In those configurations they could pull massively long trains weighing 4,000 to 7,000 tons.

The Krauss-Maffei ML4000 was 66 feet long, weighed 330,000 pounds, and generated a monumental 104,000 pounds of tractive effort. The one depicted here was painted in the yellow with black-and-white trim of the Denver & Rio Grande Western.

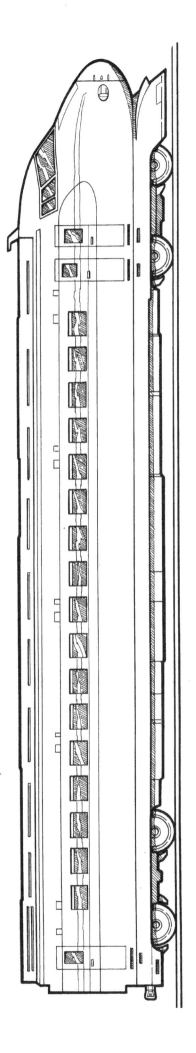

38. Japan National Railways Shinkansen (Bullet Train) 0 series. Electric trainset, 1964

Another step forward in railroad technology was made by the Japan National Railways' high-speed shinkansen ("bullet trains"). The first thirty twelve-car trainsets were brought into service on the Tokaido line in 1964, with sixty trains a day running between Tokyo and Osaka. There are now about a dozen types of shinkansen operating in hundreds of trains in various configurations on trunk lines all over Japan.

The 0 series shinkansen were the first of the bullet trains in 1964. Electric motors in the lead car and in each passenger car allowed them to cruise at 110 mph and hit speeds of 130 mph on straight stretches of track. Power was drawn from overhead lines through pantographs. A sixteen-car trainset (used between 1969 and 1999) was 1,138 feet long and weighed 2,031,200 pounds. Each car in the train including the lead cab unit had four 248-hp electric motors for a total of 15,000 hp and 103,000 pounds of tractive effort. Most bullet trains of Japan National Railways are white with either blue or green trim.

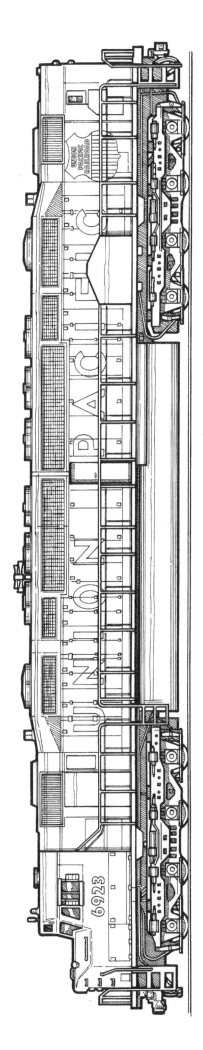

39. Union Pacific DDA40X Centennial. Diesel-electric locomotive, 1969

The third and final member of the mighty trio of Union Pacific freight locomotives is the DDA40X Centennial diesel, brought into service in 1969. With its tractive effort of 136,000 pounds, it is very close in power to the Union Pacific gas turbine engine (135,000 pounds), and the mighty Big Boy steam locomotive (137,500 pounds). The Centennial was named to commemorate the one hundred years of Union Pacific operation, dating from the driving of the golden spike at Promontory, Utah, that completed the first transcontinental railroad in 1869.

Forty-seven Centennials were built by the General Motors Electro-Motive Division between 1969 and 1971; the last was retired by 1986. The Centennial holds the record for the most powerful single-unit diesel-electric railroad engines ever operated in regular service. It is 98 feet long, weighs 545,400 pounds fully loaded with fuel, and can attain speeds of 90 mph with its two 3,300-hp engines. It wore the yellow, red, and black livery of the Union Pacific Railroad with a red, white, and blue shield emblem.

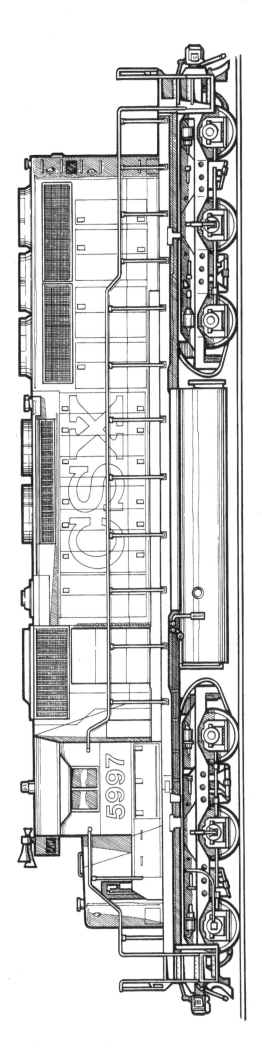

40. General Motors SD40-2. Diesel-electric locomotive, 1976

A very widely used diesel locomotive currently in service is SD40-2, manufactured by the General Motors Electro-Motive Division. In the U.S., it is used principally as freight locomotive by Conrail and CSX. By 1980 there were approximately 4,000 SD40s in operation worldwide. Subsequent more powerful models, the SD60, SD70, and SD80, have also been developed.

The SD40-2 is 68 feet long, weighs 389,000 pounds and can run at 65 mph. Its 3,000-hp diesel engine produces 87,000 pounds of tractive effort. The SD40-2 pictured here wears the blue and white livery of the CSX rail system.

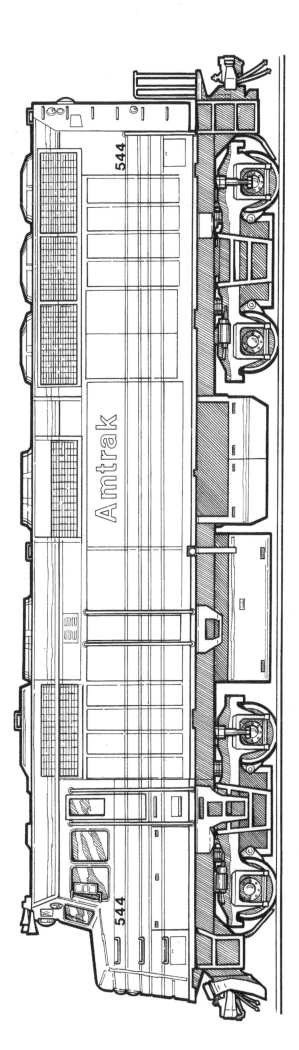

41. General Motors F40PH. Diesel-electric locomotive, 1976

The SD40's passenger-hauling partner is the F40PH, also built by the General Motors Electro-Motive Division. Introduced in 1976, the F40 is mainly used by Amtrak to pull intercity passenger trains. There are around 200 F40s in regular operation. The engine is 52 feet long and weighs 264,000 pounds. The 3,000-hp diesel power plant creates 68,440 pounds of tractive effort. The F40 can hit 100 mph but normally cruises at between 60 and 70 mph. It is shown above in the markings of the Amtrak system, which are silver with red, white, and blue trim.

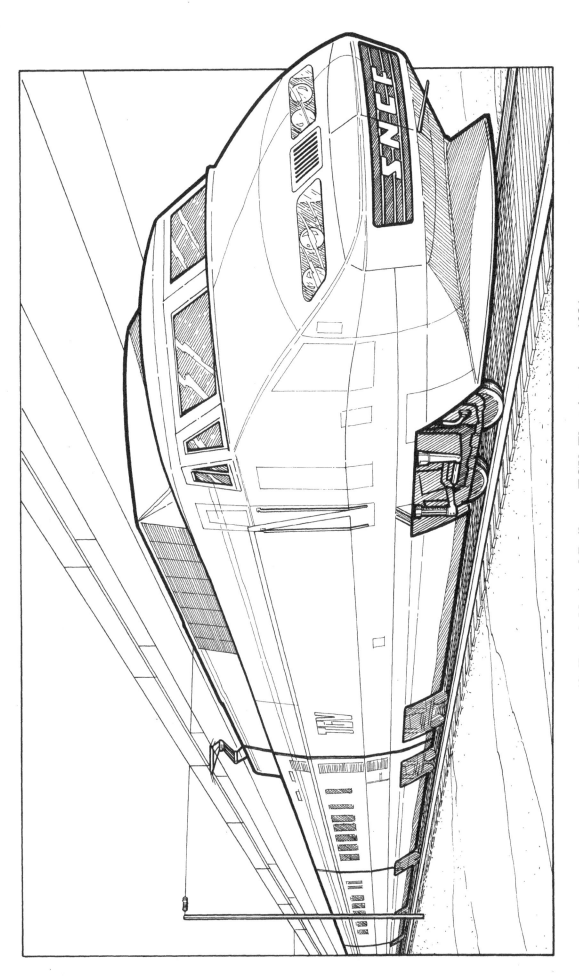

42. French National Railways TGV. Electric trainset, 1981

The current holder of the title World's Fastest Train is a TGV unit of the Société Nationale des Chemins de Fer Francais (SNCF), the French National Railways. A special five-car TGV Atlantique reached a speed of 320 mph on May 18, 1990.

"TGV" stands for *Train à Grande Vitesse,* "Fast Train." It was introduced into regular service in 1981. A TGV train typically consists of a ten-car trainset with a cab unit at each end supplying the motive power (drawn from overhead power lines through a pantograph mounted on the rear cab unit).

Pictured here is one of the earliest TGV trains of the SNCF's Paris Sud-Est division, running between Paris and Lyon. It is 656 feet long and weighs 800,000 pounds. It can cruise at 165 mph, hit 186 on straight track, and was tested on special tracks at speeds well over 200 mph. Its electric traction motors enabled it to reach such high speeds by developing 8,448 hp. The first TGVs were painted orange, gray, and white but newer versions appear in silver and blue

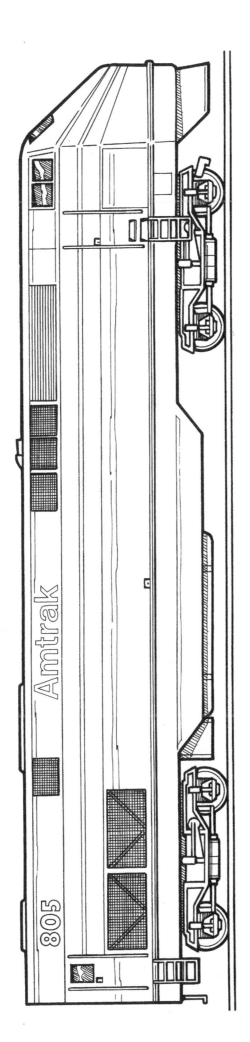

43. General Electric AMD 103 Genesis. Diesel-electric locomotive, 1993

Amtrak introduced the General Electric AMD (Amtrak Diesel) 103 diesel-electric engine in 1993 as a replacement engine for the aging F40PH. The two models in use, the P40 and its later variant, the P42, are the current standard locomotives for Amtrak passenger trains. The AMD 103's unique aerodynamic body was designed to reduce wind resistance in order to improve fuel economy. With its unusual flat-faceted styling, the AMD 103 presents a distinctive appearance among locomotives.

Designed for a maximum speed of 103 mph (hence its name), the AMD 103 P40 is powered by a 4,000-hp diesel engine (the P42's is 4,200 hp). It is 69 feet long, weighs 242,000 pounds, generates a tractive effort of 88,500 pounds, and stands a relatively tall 14½ feet high. The AMD has a fully-computerized control system in the crash-proof crew cabin. It is operated in Amtrak's silver with red and blue trim.

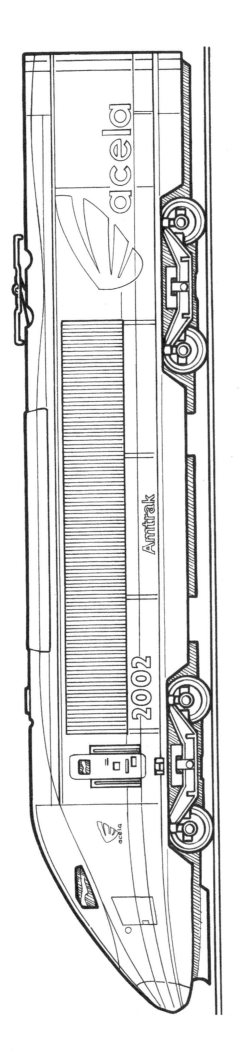

44. Amtrak Acela. Electric trainset, 2000

High-speed rail operations were begun in the United States in December of 2000 with the advent of the sleek Acela Express. Initially running only on the electrified Northeast Corridor route between Washington, D.C. and Boston, the Acela cruises at 150 mph where the track allows. The Acela's lead cab unit is 70 feet long, weighs 204,000 pounds, and develops 50,000 pounds of tractive effort. It draws electrical power from an overhead catenary cable through a pantograph. The Acela Express consists of an eight-car trainset including a power cab at each end. With its high cruising speed the Acela has cut the travel time between Boston and New York from four and a half hours to three and a half hours, and between New York and Washington from three hours to two and a half hours. Passenger satisfaction and ridership is said to be very high since the trains' introduction.

The Acela is a distant cousin of the TGV. The new trains are built by a consortium comprising the French company Alstom, designers of the TGV, and the Canadian firm Bombardier, at Bombardier facilities in Vermont and New York. The Acela wears the silver, black, and blue colors of Amtrak.